Mastering Monday.com: A Comprehensive Guide to Effective Project Management and Team Collaboration

Monday.com is a project management tool that enables users to collaborate on projects and track progress in real-time. The platform provides a visual interface for users to see all tasks and deadlines in one place, as well as who is responsible for each task. Monday.com also offers features such as chat and video conferencing, file sharing, and task dependencies.

The book covers the following:

Chapter 1: Introduction to Monday.com

1.1 Understanding the Work Operating System (Work OS) Concept

1.2 Features and Benefits of Monday.com

1.3 Navigating the Monday.com Interface

1.4 Setting Up Your Account and Customizing Your Workspace

1.5 Integrations and Extensions for Monday.com

1.6 Security and Privacy Considerations

1.7 Choosing the Right Monday.com Plan for Your Needs

1.8 Monday.com Community and Support Resources

1.9 Tips for Getting Started with Monday.com

Chapter 2: Creating and Managing Projects

2.1 Setting Up Project Boards and Workspaces

2.2 Designing Customized Boards for Different Workflows

2.3 Defining Project Goals and Objectives

Chapter 11: Security, Privacy, and Data Management in Monday.com

12.9 Harnessing the Full Potential of Monday.com

Chapter 1: Introduction to Monday.com

Monday.com is a project management tool that enables users to collaborate on projects and track progress in real-time. The platform provides a visual interface for users to see all tasks and deadlines in one place, as well as who is responsible for each task. Monday.com also offers features such as chat and video conferencing, file sharing, and task dependencies.

1.1 Understanding the Work Operating System (Work OS) Concept

The Work Operating System (Work OS) concept is a framework that can be used to guide the development of work systems. It is based on the belief that work systems should be designed to support the work that people do, rather than the other way around.

The Work OS concept has three key components:

1. The work system should be designed around the needs of the people who use it.

2. The work system should be designed to be flexible and adaptable, so that it can change as the needs of the people who use it change.

3. The work system should be designed to be understandable and transparent, so that people can see how it works and why it works the way it does.

1.2 Features and Benefits of Monday.com

Monday.com is a project management software that helps teams plan, track, and collaborate on their work. It offers a variety of features and benefits that make it an effective tool for managing projects of all sizes.

Some of the key features of Monday.com include:

- A visual project management interface that makes it easy to see what work needs to be done and who is responsible for it
- The ability to create custom workflows to match the unique needs of your project
- A variety of integrations with popular productivity tools, such as Google Drive, Slack, and Zapier

- A robust permissions system that allows you to control who has access to which parts of your project
- A mobile app that allows you to stay connected to your project even when you're on the go

The benefits of using Monday.com include:

- Increased productivity and efficiency: Monday.com helps teams work together more effectively by giving them a clear overview of what needs to be done and who is responsible for it.
- Improved communication and collaboration: The visual interface and variety of integrations make it easy for team members to stay in sync and share information.
- Greater flexibility and control: The custom workflows and permissions system give you the ability to tailor the software to your specific needs and control who has access to which parts of your project.
- Increased visibility and transparency: The mobile app and activity feed provide you with visibility into what's happening with your project even when you're not at your desk.

Monday.com is a cloud-based project management software that enables users to collaborate on projects and tasks in real-time. The software provides a variety of features and tools to help users manage their projects, including a drag-and-drop interface, Gantt charts, kanban boards, and more.

The Monday.com interface is designed to be user-friendly and intuitive. The main navigation bar is located at the top of the screen and includes options for Projects, Tasks, Calendar, Inbox, and more. The left sidebar provides quick access to your projects, kanban boards, and Gantt charts. The right sidebar contains a search bar and options for filtering and sorting your data.

The Projects page is the default landing page when you first login to Monday.com. This page provides an overview of all your projects, as well as any recent activity. You can also create new projects from this page.

The Tasks page enables you to view and manage all your tasks in one place. This page includes a variety of features and tools to help you stay organized, including a drag-and-drop interface, Gantt charts, and kanban boards.

The Calendar page provides a visual overview of your tasks and deadlines. This page includes a variety of features and tools to help you stay on track, including a drag-and-drop interface, Gantt charts, and kanban boards.

The Inbox is a central location for all your notifications and messages. This page includes a variety of features and tools to help you stay on top of your projects, including a drag-and-drop interface, Gantt charts, and kanban boards.

1.4 Setting Up Your Monday.com Account and Customizing Your Workspace

Setting Up Your Monday.com Account and Customizing Your Workspace

Monday.com is a powerful project management tool that can help you stay organized and on track with your work. In order to get the most out of Monday.com, it is important to set up your account and customize your workspace to fit your specific needs.

To set up your Monday.com account, simply go to the website and create a new account. You will need to provide your name, email address, and create a password. Once you have created your account, you can then begin to customize your workspace.

There are a few things that you can do to customize your workspace, such as:

1. Choose the color scheme that you want to use.

2. Select the font size and style that you prefer.

3. Choose the layout that you want to use for your workspace.

4. Add or remove any widgets that you want.

5. Set up your preferences for how you want your workspace to function.

Once you have customized your workspace, you can then begin to add projects and tasks. To do this, simply click on the "Add Project" or "Add Task" button and fill out the necessary information.

You can also invite other users to collaborate on projects with you by clicking on the "Invite" button. This will allow you to enter their email address and send them an invitation to join your workspace.

Monday.com is a powerful tool that can help you stay organized and on track with your work. By taking the time to set up your account and customize your workspace, you can ensure that you are getting the most out of the tool.

1.5 Integrations and Extensions for Monday.com

Monday.com offers a variety of integrations and extensions to help users customize their experience and get the most out of the platform. Integrations are available for a variety of popular applications and services, including Google Drive, Dropbox, and OneDrive. Extensions provide additional functionality and customization options for Monday.com users.

1.6 Security and Privacy Considerations in Monday.com

There are a number of security and privacy considerations to take into account when using Monday.com. First and foremost, all data stored in Monday.com is encrypted at rest, so that it can only be accessed by authorized users. In addition, Monday.com offers a number of features to help users keep their data safe, such as two-factor authentication and the ability to set up password-protected sharing links.

Monday.com also takes data privacy seriously, and offers a number of features to help users control who has access to their data. For example, users can choose to share data only with specific users, or to keep data private and only allow access to it on a need-to-know basis.

Finally, it is important to note that Monday.com is compliant with a number of data privacy laws and regulations, including the EU General Data Protection Regulation (GDPR).

1.7 Choosing the Right Monday.com Plan for Your Needs

There are four different Monday.com plans: Starter, Pro, Enterprise, and Custom. The Starter plan is the most basic and includes limited features and integrations. The Pro plan includes more features and integrations, as well as unlimited users. The Enterprise plan includes all features and integrations, as well as unlimited users and custom branding. The Custom plan is customized to the specific needs of the customer.

The best plan for a customer depends on their needs. If a customer only needs the most basic features, then the Starter plan would be sufficient. If a customer needs more features and integrations, then the Pro plan would be a better option. If a customer needs all features and integrations, as well as unlimited users and custom branding, then the Enterprise plan would be the best option. If a customer's needs are not met by any of the other plans, then the Custom plan would be the best option.

1.8 Monday.com Community and Support Resources

The Monday.com Community and Support Resources are a great way to get help and support for using Monday.com. There are forums, a knowledge base, and live chat support available. The community forums are a great place to ask questions and get help from other Monday.com users. The knowledge base has articles on how to use Monday.com, troubleshooting, and FAQs. Live chat support is available Monday-Friday 9am-5pm EST.

Monday.com is a project management tool that helps teams stay organized and efficient.

Here are 9 tips to help you get started with Monday.com:

1. Create a custom workspace for your team. This will help everyone stay on the same page and avoid confusion.

2. Add your team members to the workspace. This way, everyone will have access to the same information and can collaborate effectively.

3. Create columns and rows to organize your data. This will help you keep track of tasks, deadlines, and other important information.

4. Use the kanban view to visualize your workflows. This will help you see what needs to be done and when it needs to be done.

5. Use the calendar view to track deadlines and milestones. This will help you stay on track and avoid missing important deadlines.

6. Use the Gantt chart view to plan and track complex projects. This will help you see the big

picture and ensure that all tasks are completed on time.

7. Use the map view to track location-based data. This can be helpful for tracking deliveries, service calls, and other data that has a geographic component.

8. Use the reporting features to generate custom reports. This will help you track progress and identify areas where improvements can be made.

9. Use the integrations to connect Monday.com with other tools. This will help you automate tasks and keep all of your data in one place.

Chapter 2: Creating and Managing Projects in Monday.com

2.1 Setting Up Project Boards and Workspaces in Monday.com

Monday.com is a project management tool that allows users to create and manage projects through a variety of features, including project boards and workspaces. In order to set up a project board, users first need to create a workspace. Once a workspace has been created, users can add projects to the workspace by clicking the "Add Project" button.

Project boards can be used to track the progress of projects and to see which tasks need to be completed. To create a project board, users first need to create a workspace and then add projects to the workspace. Once projects have been added, users can click on the "Board" tab and then click the "Create Board" button.

In order to add tasks to a project board, users first need to create a workspace and then add projects to the workspace. Once projects have been added, users can click on the "Board" tab and then click on the "Add Task" button. Tasks can be assigned to specific users and can be given due dates.

Project boards can be used to track the progress of projects and to see which tasks need to be completed. To create a project board, users first need to create a workspace and then add projects to the workspace. Once projects have been added, users can click on the "Board" tab and then click the "Create Board" button.

In order to add tasks to a project board, users first need to create a workspace and then add projects to the workspace. Once projects have been added, users can click on the "Board" tab and then click on the "Add Task" button. Tasks can be assigned to specific users and can be given due dates.

2.2 Designing Customized Boards in Monday.com for Different Workflows

Monday.com's board feature is very versatile and can be customized to fit a variety of different workflows. In this chapter, we will go over how to design a customized board in Monday.com for different workflows.

First, you will need to decide what kind of workflow you would like to create. There are many different types of workflows that can be created in Monday.com, so it is important to choose one that will fit your needs.

Once you have decided on the type of workflow you would like to create, you will need to design your board. To do this, you will need to add columns and rows to your board. You can add as many or as few columns and rows as you like.

Once you have added columns and rows to your board, you can then start adding tasks to your board. To do this, you will need to click on the "Add task" button.

Once you have added a task to your board, you can then assign that task to a specific person. To do this, you will need to click on the "Assign" button.

Once you have assigned a task to a specific person, you can then add details to that task. To do this, you will need to click on the "Add details" button.

Once you have added details to a task, you can then add comments to that task. To do this, you will need to click on the "Add comment" button.

Once you have added comments to a task, you can then add attachments to that task. To do this, you will need to click on the "Add attachment" button.

Once you have added attachments to a task, you can then add labels to that task. To do this, you will need to click on the "Add label" button.

Once you have added labels to a task, you can then add due dates to that task. To do this, you will need to click on the "Add due date" button.

Once you have added due dates to a task, you can then add reminders to that task. To do this, you will need to click on the "Add reminder" button.

Once you have added reminders to a task, you can then add notes to that task. To do this, you will need to click on the "Add note" button.

Once you have added notes to a task, you can then add links to that task. To do this, you will need to click on the "Add link" button.

Once you have added links to a task, you can then add files to that task. To do this, you will need to click on the "Add file" button.

Once you have added files to a task, you can then add comments to that task. To do this, you will need to click on the "Add comment" button.

Once you have added comments to a task, you can then add attachments to that task. To do this, you will need to click on the "Add attachment" button.

Once you have added attachments to a task, you can then add labels to that task. To do this, you will need to click on the "Add label" button.

Once you have added labels to a task, you can then add due dates to that task. To do this, you will need to click on the "Add due date" button.

Once you have added due dates to a task, you can then add reminders to that task. To do this, you will need to click on the "Add reminder" button.

Once you have added reminders to a task, you can then add notes to that task. To do this, you will need to click on the "Add note" button.

Once you have added notes to a task, you can then add links to that task. To do this, you will need to click on the "Add link" button.

Once you have added links to a task, you can then add files to that task. To do this, you will need to click on the "Add file" button.

2.3 Defining Project Goals and Objectives in Monday.com

Monday.com's project management software is designed to help teams achieve their goals and objectives. When creating a new project, teams can define their goals and objectives in the project settings. This ensures that everyone is aware of the project's purpose and what needs to be accomplished.

The project goals and objectives can be updated at any time, giving teams the flexibility to adjust their plans as needed. Monday.com also offers a variety of features to help teams track their progress and stay on track. For example, teams can create task lists, set deadlines, and assign tasks to specific team members. Progress can be monitored in the project's activity feed, and team members can leave comments and feedback on tasks.

2.4 Creating and Assigning Tasks in Monday.com

Monday.com is a project management tool that helps teams track and manage their work. One of the features of Monday.com is the ability to create and assign tasks.

Creating a task in Monday.com is simple. First, click on the "Add a task" button. This will open up a new task window. In this window, you will enter the task name, description, and due date. You can also assign the task to a specific team member.

Once you have created the task, it will appear in the "My Tasks" section of Monday.com. From here, you can view and manage your tasks. To mark a task as complete, simply click on the checkmark next to the task.

Assigning tasks in Monday.com is just as easy. First, click on the "Assign" button next to the task. This will open up a new window where you can select the team member you would like to assign the task to. Once you have selected the team member, click on the "Assign" button.

The team member you assigned the task to will now be able to view the task in their "My Tasks" section. They can also mark the task as complete from here.

2.5 Setting Due Dates and Prioritizing Tasks in Monday.com

Monday.com offers users the ability to set due dates and prioritize tasks in order to better manage their projects. To set a due date, users simply need to click on the task and then click on the "Set Due Date" option. From there, users can select the date and time that they would like the task to be due. Once the due date is set, the task will be automatically added to the user's calendar.

Prioritizing tasks in Monday.com is just as easy. To do so, users simply need to click on the task and then click on the "Prioritize" option. From there, users can select the priority level that they would like to assign to the task. The three priority levels are high, medium, and low. By default, all tasks are set to the medium priority level.

Both due dates and task priorities can be helpful when it comes to managing projects in Monday.com. Due dates can help to ensure that tasks are completed by a certain date and time, while task priorities can help to ensure that the most important tasks are completed first.

2.6 Using Tags, Labels, and Statuses to Track Progress in Monday.com

Monday.com offers a variety of ways to track progress on projects. One way is to use tags, labels, and statuses.

Tags are a way to categorize items in Monday.com. They can be used to track progress on projects by tagging items with the project name. For example, if you are working on a project called "Website redesign," you could tag all of the items related to that project with the tag "website redesign." This would allow you to easily find all of the items related to the project and see the progress that has been made.

Labels are another way to categorize items in Monday.com. They can be used to track progress on projects by labeling items with the project name. For example, if you are working on a project called "Website redesign," you could label all of the items related to that project with the label "website redesign." This would allow you to easily find all of the items related to the project and see the progress that has been made.

Statuses are a way to track the progress of items in Monday.com. They can be used to track progress on projects by setting the status of items to "In Progress," "Completed," or "On Hold." For example, if you are working on a project called "Website redesign," you could set the status of all of the items related to that project to "In Progress." This would allow you to easily see which items are still in progress and which have been completed.

Tags, labels, and statuses are just a few of the ways that you can track progress on projects in Monday.com. You can also use other features, such as the Gantt chart, to track progress.

2.7 Collaborating with Team Members on Projects in Monday.com

Monday.com is a great tool for collaborating with team members on projects. With its easy-to-use interface, you can easily add and manage team members, as well as create and assign tasks. You can also track the progress of your project with its built-in project management features.

2.8 Sharing and Access Permissions for Projects in Monday.com

Monday.com's sharing and access permissions for projects is a great way to control who can see and edit your project. By default, only the project owner can see and edit the project, but you can change the permissions for each project member individually.

To change the permissions for a project member, go to the project's settings page and click on the "Members" tab. Then, click on the member's name and select the "Edit" button.

In the "Edit Member" pop-up, you can change the member's role to either "Owner", "Admin", or "Member". You can also select whether or not the member can see the project's tasks, files, and comments.

If you want to give a member access to only certain tasks in the project, you can select the "Tasks" tab and then click on the "Edit" button next to the member's name. In the "Edit Tasks" pop-up, you can select which tasks the member can see and edit.

Monday.com's sharing and access permissions for projects is a great way to make sure that only the people who need to see and edit your project can do so. By default, only the project owner can see and edit the project, but you can change the permissions for each project member individually. This ensures that your project is only seen and edited by the people who need to see and edit it, and that no one else can access it.

2.9 Leveraging Templates for Efficient Project Setup in Monday.com

Monday.com's project templates feature is a great way to save time and ensure consistency when setting up new projects. When creating a new project, simply select the "use a template" option, then choose from a variety of pre-built templates, or create your own custom template.

Templates can be customized to include the specific tasks, columns, and workflows that are relevant to your project. This makes it easy to get started on a new project, and ensures that all of the necessary information is captured from the start.

Monday.com's project templates are a great way to save time and ensure consistency when setting up new projects. By using a template, you can be sure that all of the necessary information is captured from the start, and that the project is set up in a way that is most efficient for your team.

Chapter 3: Visualizing and Tracking Project Progress in Monday.com

3.1 Utilizing Different Views in Monday.com: Kanban, Calendar, Gantt Charts

Monday.com offers three ways to view your project data: Kanban, Calendar, and Gantt Charts.

Kanban:

The Kanban view is a great way to see an overview of your project and get a sense of what needs to be done. You can see all of the tasks in your project and who is responsible for each one. This view is also helpful for seeing what tasks are dependent on each other.

Calendar:

The Calendar view is helpful for seeing when tasks are due and for planning your project timeline. You can see all of the tasks in your project and when they are due. This view is also helpful for seeing which tasks are dependent on each other.

Gantt Charts:

Gantt charts are a great way to see an overview of your project and get a sense of what needs to be done. You can see all of the tasks in your project and who is responsible for each one. This view is also helpful for seeing what tasks are dependent on each other.

3.2 Visualizing Task Dependencies and Timelines in Monday.com

Monday.com is a project management tool that allows users to visualize task dependencies and timelines. This is helpful in understanding how tasks are related to each other and how they fit into the overall project timeline. Users can see at a glance which tasks are dependent on others, and can plan accordingly. This feature is also helpful for tracking project progress, as users can see which tasks have been completed and which are still outstanding.

3.3 Tracking Progress with Milestones and Deadlines in Monday.com

Monday.com's "Visualizing and Tracking Project Progress" chapter explains how to use milestones and deadlines to track progress on your projects.

Milestones are used to mark significant events or accomplishments on a project, and can be used to track progress towards a goal. Deadlines are used to set a date by which a task must be completed, and can be used to ensure that tasks are completed on time.

Both milestones and deadlines can be added to tasks in Monday.com, and can be used to track progress on a project. To add a milestone or deadline to a task, click on the task and then click on the "Add milestone or deadline" button.

Milestones and deadlines can be used to track progress on a project in Monday.com. By adding milestones and deadlines to tasks, you can see at a glance what needs to be done and when it needs to be done. This helps you to stay on track and ensure that your project is completed on time.

3.4 Using Progress Indicators and Status Updates in Monday.com

Monday.com's progress indicators and status updates help you visualize and track the progress of your projects. By using these features, you can stay up-to-date on the status of your projects, and ensure that your team is on track to meet your deadlines.

Progress indicators provide an at-a-glance view of the status of your projects. You can use them to track the progress of individual tasks, or to see how close your team is to completing a project. Monday.com's progress indicators are customizable, so you can choose the colors and icons that best represent your projects.

Status updates give you more information about the progress of your projects. You can use them to see which tasks are on track, and which ones are behind schedule. Status updates can also be used to communicate changes to your team, or to provide feedback on a project.

3.5 Filtering and Sorting Data for Clear Visibility in Monday.com

Monday.com is a flexible, visual project management tool that helps teams track progress and manage projects easily. One of the most powerful features of Monday.com is its ability to filter and sort data for clear visibility. This is especially useful when tracking project progress, as it allows users to quickly see which tasks are on track, behind schedule, or at risk.

There are a few different ways to filter and sort data in Monday.com. The first is by using the built-in filters. These filters can be found in the left-hand sidebar, and they allow users to narrow down the data displayed in the main view. For example, users can filter by task status, due date, assignee, or tag.

The second way to filter and sort data is by using the search bar. The search bar is located at the top of the page, and it allows users to search for specific tasks or keywords. For example, users can search for all tasks that are due in the next week, or all tasks that are assigned to a specific person.

The third way to filter and sort data is by using the views. Views are located in the top-right corner of the page, and they allow users to customize the data displayed in the main view. For example, users can create a view that only displays tasks that are due in the next week.

Monday.com also offers a few different ways to sort data. The first is by using the built-in sorting options. These options can be found in the left-hand sidebar, and they allow users to sort tasks by due date, priority, or status.

The second way to sort data is by using the search bar. The search bar is located at the top of the page, and it allows users to sort tasks by keyword. For example, users can search for all tasks that are due in the next week, or all tasks that are assigned to a specific person.

The third way to sort data is by using the views. Views are located in the top-right corner of the page, and they allow users to sort tasks by due date, priority, or status.

Monday.com also offers a few different ways to visualize data. The first is by using the built-in charts. These charts can be found in the left-hand sidebar, and they allow users to see a visual representation of the data. For example, users can see a pie chart that shows the percentage of tasks that are on track, behind schedule, or at risk.

The second way to visualize data is by using the search bar. The search bar is located at the top of the page, and it allows users to visualize tasks by keyword. For example, users can search for all tasks that are due in the next week, or all tasks that are assigned to a specific person.

The third way to visualize data is by using the views. Views are located in the top-right corner of the page, and they allow users to visualize tasks by due date, priority, or status.

3.6 Customizing Views and Reports in Monday.com

Monday.com offers a variety of ways to customize views and reports to fit the specific needs of your team or project. In this section, we'll cover some of the most common ways to customize views and reports in Monday.com.

One way to customize views and reports in Monday.com is to use the "Columns" and "Rows" options to rearrange the order of information. For example, you can use the "Columns" option to move the "Due Date" column to the far left side of the screen, so it's always visible. Or, you can use the "Rows" option to organize tasks by priority, so the most important tasks are always at the top of the list.

Another way to customize views and reports is to use the "Filters" option to only display the information that's most relevant to you. For example, you can use the "Filters" option to only show tasks that are due in the next 7 days, or only show tasks that are assigned to you.

Finally, you can use the "Group By" option to group information together in a way that makes sense for your team or project. For example, you can use the "Group By" option to group tasks by project, so all of the tasks for a particular project are grouped together.

These are just a few of the ways you can customize views and reports in Monday.com. By using these options, you can tailor the information displayed in Monday.com to fit the specific needs of your team or project.

3.7 Monitoring Workload and Resource Allocation in Monday.com

Monday.com's workload and resource allocation monitoring tools allow users to see how much work is being done by each team member and how resources are being used. This information can be used to identify areas where work is not being evenly distributed or where resources are being underutilized. It can also help to identify potential bottlenecks in the project's progress.

3.8 Analyzing Project Analytics and Metrics in Monday.com

Monday.com's project analytics and metrics features allow users to see how their projects are progressing and identify areas that need improvement. The features include a variety of charts and graphs that can be customized to show different data sets, as well as a project health report that gives an overview of the project's status. Users can also set up alerts to notify them of changes in the project's analytics.

3.9 Exporting and Sharing Project Reports in Monday.com

Monday.com offers a variety of ways to export and share project reports. Reports can be exported as PDFs, images, or CSV files. They can also be shared via email, link, or embedded on a website or blog.

To export a report, click the export icon in the upper right corner of the report. This will open a menu of export options.

To share a report, click the share icon in the upper right corner of the report. This will open a menu of share options.

Email:

Click the email icon to open your default email client with a link to the report already inserted. Add any additional message you would like and click send.

Link:

Click the link icon to copy a link to the report to your clipboard. This link can be pasted into an email, chat, or any other text field.

Embed:

Click the embed icon to open a dialog with the HTML code needed to embed the report on a website or blog. Copy the code and paste it into the desired location on your website or blog.

Chapter 4: Streamlining Collaboration and Communication in Monday.com

4.1 Communicating with Team Members on Monday.com

Monday.com is a great tool for team communication and collaboration. It allows team members to easily communicate with each other and stay organized. Monday.com makes it easy to stay on top of tasks and projects, and to keep everyone on the same page.

4.2 Utilizing the Inbox and Notifications in Monday.com

Monday.com's Inbox and Notifications feature is a great way to keep track of your team's progress and activity. By subscribing to notifications, you can receive updates on your team's progress and activity in real-time, which can be a valuable way to stay informed and up-to-date on your team's work. Additionally, the Inbox can be used as a way to quickly and easily access important information and files that have been shared with you.

4.3 Integrating Communication Tools (Slack, Microsoft Teams) in Monday.com

Monday.com's integration with communication tools like Slack and Microsoft Teams allows users to streamline their collaboration and communication. By integrating Monday.com with these tools, users can easily send messages, files, and tasks between Monday.com and their communication tool of choice. This integration makes it easy for users to keep track of their work in one place, and makes communication and collaboration between team members simpler and more efficient.

4.4 Commenting and Mentioning Team Members in Monday.com

Monday.com offers a variety of ways to comment on and mention team members in items. To comment on an item, simply click the "Add a comment" button at the bottom of the item. This will open a text box where you can type your comment. To mention a team member, simply type "@" followed by their name. This will bring up a

list of team members that you can select from.
Once you've selected the team member you want
to mention, their name will be inserted into the
comment box. You can then continue typing your
comment.

Mentioning team members in comments is a great
way to get their attention and make sure they see
your comment. It's also a great way to start a
conversation or get feedback from team members.
If you're ever unsure about something, mention a
team member in a comment and ask for their
opinion. This is a great way to get input from
others and make sure everyone is on the same
page.

4.5 Collaborative Document Editing and File Sharing in Monday.com

Monday.com's collaborative document editing and
file sharing features streamline collaboration and
communication by allowing users to work on
documents and files together in real time. This
makes it easy to track changes and ensure that
everyone is on the same page, which can save time
and reduce frustration when working on projects
as a team.Monday.com's document editor includes
a number of features that make collaboration easy,

such as the ability to @mention other users to get their attention, leave comments on specific sections of a document, and see who else is currently viewing or editing the document. Files can be easily shared with other users by simply sending a link, and users can also give others the ability to edit the file or add their own comments. Monday.com's file sharing features make it easy to keep track of all the files associated with a project in one place, and make it easy to find the most recent version of a file.

4.6 Managing Document Versions and Revisions in Monday.com

Monday.com's document management features allow users to easily create, track, and manage versions and revisions of documents within the platform. Users can create new versions of documents with just a few clicks, and can track and manage revisions using the platform's built-in revision history feature. Monday.com also makes it easy to share documents with others, and to collaborate on documents in real-time.

4.7 Conducting Discussions and Brainstorming Sessions in Monday.com

Monday.com is a great tool for conducting discussions and brainstorming sessions. The platform is designed to facilitate collaboration and communication between team members. Monday.com makes it easy to create and manage discussion threads, and to track and monitor the progress of discussions. The platform also provides tools for team members to share files and ideas, and to vote on ideas.

4.8 Coordinating Meetings and Scheduling in Monday.com

Monday.com is a great tool for coordinating meetings and scheduling. With Monday.com, you can easily create and manage meetings, invite participants, and track meeting progress. You can also use Monday.com to schedule meeting times, locations, and agenda items. Monday.com makes it easy to stay on top of meeting logistics and ensure that meetings run smoothly.

4.9 Enhancing Remote Collaboration with Monday.com

Monday.com is a great tool for enhancing remote collaboration. With Monday.com, team members can easily stay up-to-date on project progress, communicate with each other, and track tasks. Monday.com makes it easy to keep everyone on the same page and helps to improve communication and collaboration.

Chapter 5: Automating Workflows and Processes in Monday.com

5.1 Understanding Automation Capabilities in Monday.com

Monday.com's automation capabilities are designed to streamline workflows and processes by automating repetitive tasks. With automation, users can define rules that trigger certain actions to occur automatically when specific conditions are met. This can save time and effort by eliminating the need to manually perform these tasks.

There are two types of automation that can be used in Monday.com: workflows and recipes. Workflows are designed to automate tasks that are performed regularly, such as sending a weekly report or updating a customer database. Recipes are designed to automate more complex processes that involve multiple steps and tasks.

To create an automation, users first need to identify the trigger, which is the event that will initiate the automation. Once the trigger is defined, the user can then specify the actions that should occur automatically. These actions can be performed by Monday.com itself, or they can be integrated with third-party applications.

Monday.com offers a wide range of pre-built automation templates, or users can create their own custom automation. Automations can be turned on or off at any time, and they can be edited or deleted as needed.

Automations can be a great way to improve efficiency and productivity in Monday.com. By taking care of repetitive tasks automatically, users can focus on more important work. Automations can also help to ensure that tasks are completed accurately and on time.

5.2 Setting Up Automated Notifications and Reminders in Monday.com

Monday.com's Automated Notifications and Reminders feature allows you to set up notifications and reminders for tasks, events, or deadlines that are coming up in your workflows. This can be a great way to stay on top of your work and make sure that nothing falls through the cracks.

To set up Automated Notifications and Reminders, go to the Automation tab in your account settings. From here, you can create a new Automation rule by clicking on the "New Rule" button.

In the "Rule Details" section, you will need to give your rule a name and description. You will also need to choose when the rule should be triggered. For Automated Notifications and Reminders, you will want to choose the "Task is due" trigger.

In the "Actions" section, you will need to choose what action should be taken when the rule is triggered. For Automated Notifications and Reminders, you will want to choose the "Send email" action.

In the "Recipients" section, you will need to choose who should receive the notification or reminder. You can choose to send the notification or reminder to the assignee of the task, the creator of the task, or a specific email address.

In the "Message" section, you will need to write the message that should be sent in the notification or reminder. You can use merge fields to personalize the message for each recipient.

In the "Send Options" section, you will need to choose how often the notification or reminder should be sent. You can choose to send the notification or reminder immediately, or you can choose to send it a certain number of days, hours, or minutes before the task is due.

Once you have finished setting up your Automated Notification or Reminder, click on the "Create Rule" button to save it.

5.3 Creating Workflow Automation with Triggers and Actions in Monday.com

Monday.com's workflow automation feature allows you to create triggers and actions that will automatically move items through your workflow. For example, you could create a trigger that automatically moves an item to the "In Progress" column when the item's due date is reached. Or you could create an action that automatically sends an email notification when an item is moved to the "Completed" column.

To create a workflow automation, click the "Automate" button at the top of your board. This will open the workflow automation builder.

First, you will need to choose a trigger. A trigger is an event that will cause the automation to run. For example, you could choose the "Item is created" trigger, which will cause the automation to run whenever an item is added to the board.

Next, you will need to choose an action. An action is something that will happen when the trigger is fired. For example, you could choose the "Send email" action, which will send an email notification when the trigger is fired.

Finally, you will need to specify any conditions that must be met for the automation to run. For example, you could specify that the automation should only run when the item's due date is reached.

Once you have configured the trigger, action, and conditions, click the "Create Automation" button to save the automation.

5.4 Streamlining Task Assignment and Approval Processes in Monday.com

Monday.com's streamlined task assignment and approval processes help users save time and increase efficiency by automating workflows and processes.Monday.com's streamlined task assignment and approval processes help users save time and increase efficiency by automating workflows and processes.Monday.com's streamlined task assignment and approval processes include the following features:

- Automated task assignment: Tasks can be automatically assigned to users based on pre-defined criteria such as skills, availability, or location.

- Automated task approval: Tasks can be automatically approved based on pre-defined criteria such as completion of all required tasks, approval by all required users, or passage of a certain amount of time.

- Automated email notifications: Users can be automatically notified via email when tasks are assigned, approved, or completed.

- Automated task tracking: Tasks can be automatically tracked and monitored for progress and completion.

5.5 Using Custom Automations to Save Time in Monday.com

Monday.com's Custom Automations feature allows users to create and save time by automating tasks and processes within the app. This can be done by creating a custom automation rule, which can be triggered by a specific event or action, and then specifying the actions that should be taken automatically in response. For example, a user could create a rule that automatically creates a new task in a specific project whenever a new customer is created in the CRM system. This would save the user from having to manually create the task each time, and would ensure that it is always created in the correct project. Custom automation rules can be created for any process or task that is regularly performed in Monday.com, and can be customized to fit the specific needs of the user or organization.

5.6 Integration-Based Automations with Other Tools in Monday.com

Monday.com's integration-based automations allow users to connect their Monday.com account with other tools and services in order to automate workflows and processes. This can be done through the use of Zapier, IFTTT, or Microsoft Flow. By connecting Monday.com with other tools, users can automate tasks such as creating new items in Monday.com based on trigger events from other tools, updating items in Monday.com based on changes made in other tools, or creating alerts and notifications based on activity in Monday.com.

5.7 Monitoring and Troubleshooting Automations in Monday.com

Monday.com's automation feature is a great way to streamline workflows and processes. However, as with any automation, there is always the potential for things to go wrong. That's why it's important to monitor and troubleshoot automations on a regular basis.

There are a few different ways to monitor automations in Monday.com. The first is to check the automation log. This log will show you all of the automations that have been run, as well as any errors that may have occurred.

Another way to monitor automations is to use the "Test" feature. This feature allows you to test an automation before it is actually run. This is a great way to make sure that an automation is working correctly before it is put into production.

If an automation does fail, there are a few different ways to troubleshoot the issue. First, you can check the automation log to see if there are any error messages. This can help you to identify the cause of the problem.

Another way to troubleshoot automations is to use the "Debug" feature. This feature allows you to step through an automation to see what is happening at each step. This can be a great way to identify where the problem is occurring.

Finally, if all else fails, you can always contact Monday.com support. They will be able to help you troubleshoot the issue and get your automation up and running again.

5.8 Advanced Automation Techniques and Best Practices in Monday.com

Monday.com's advanced automation techniques and best practices allow users to automate workflows and processes quickly and easily. By automating workflows and processes, users can save time and increase efficiency. Monday.com's automation features include:

1. Automated workflows: Monday.com's automated workflows allow users to automatically create and manage workflows. Automated workflows can be created for any process or task, and can be customized to fit the needs of any organization.

2. Process management: Monday.com's process management features allow users to manage and automate processes quickly and easily. Monday.com's process management features include:

3. Task management: Monday.com's task management features allow users to manage and automate tasks quickly and easily. Monday.com's task management features include:

4. Reporting: Monday.com's reporting features allow users to track and report on the progress of their workflows and processes. Monday.com's reporting features include:

5. Best practices: Monday.com's best practices allow users to optimize their workflows and processes. Monday.com's best practices include:

By using Monday.com's advanced automation techniques and best practices, users can save time and increase efficiency.

5.9 Optimizing Workflows for Efficiency and Productivity in Monday.com

Monday.com's workflow automation features can help optimize your team's efficiency and productivity. By automating tasks and processes, you can free up time for your team to focus on more important work. In addition, automating tasks can help ensure that work is completed accurately and on time.

There are a few ways to automate tasks in Monday.com. One way is to use the Automations feature. With Automations, you can create rules that automatically trigger certain actions when certain conditions are met. For example, you could create a rule that automatically assigns a task to a specific team member when the task is created.

Another way to automate tasks is to use the Zapier integration. Zapier is a third-party service that allows you to connect Monday.com with over 1,000 other apps. With Zapier, you can automate tasks such as creating tasks in Monday.com when new items are added to a Google Sheets spreadsheet.

To learn more about automating tasks in Monday.com, check out the following resources:

- Automations Overview
- How to Use Automations
- Zapier Integration Overview
- How to Use the Zapier Integration

Chapter 6: Advanced Features and Functionality in Monday.com

6.1 Creating Dependencies and Relationships Between Tasks in Monday.com

Monday.com offers a variety of ways to create dependencies and relationships between tasks. One way is to create a dependency directly between two tasks. To do this, simply click on the task you want to be dependent on, then click the "Depends on" button at the top of the task's detail pane.

This will bring up a menu of all the tasks in the same project that the first task depends on. Simply select the task you want to create a dependency with and click the "Add Dependency" button.

Another way to create dependencies is to use the "Dependencies" column in the project kanban view. To do this, simply click on the "Dependencies" column header and then drag and drop the task you want to be dependent on into the column of the task you want to create the dependency with.

You can also create relationships between tasks using the "Relationships" column in the project kanban view. To do this, simply click on the "Relationships" column header and then drag and drop the task you want to be related to into the column of the task you want to create the relationship with.

Both dependencies and relationships can be managed from the "Dependencies & Relationships" tab of the task detail pane. Here you can see all the tasks a given task is dependent on or related to, as well as all the tasks that depend on or are related to a given task. You can also add, remove, or edit dependencies and relationships from this tab.

6.2 Utilizing Formula Columns for Dynamic Calculations in Monday.com

Monday.com's formula column feature is an incredibly powerful tool that allows users to dynamically calculate values based on the data entered into other columns in the same row. This can be extremely useful for things like tracking project progress, budgeting, and more.

To create a formula column, simply click the "Add Column" button at the top of your board and select

"Formula." Then, you'll need to specify what kind of calculation you want to perform. Monday.com offers a wide variety of options, including basic arithmetic, conditional statements, and lookup functions.

Once you've selected the appropriate calculation, you can then specify which columns you want to include in the calculation. For each column, you can also specify whether you want to use the column's value or the column's label.

Once you've saved your formula column, it will automatically update whenever the values in the other columns change. This makes it easy to keep your board up-to-date without having to manually recalculate values.

Formula columns can be an extremely valuable tool for Monday.com users. They can save you time by allowing you to automatically calculate values, and they can provide valuable insights by allowing you to dynamically track data.

6.3 Using Time Tracking and Resource Allocation Features in Monday.com

Monday.com's time tracking and resource allocation features are some of the most robust and customizable on the market. With these features, users can track time spent on tasks, allocate resources based on task difficulty, and view detailed reports on time and resource usage.

Monday.com's time tracking features are designed to be as flexible as possible. Users can start and stop the timer for a task at any time, add manual entries for time spent on a task, and set up recurring timers for tasks that need to be completed on a regular basis. Monday.com also offers a variety of ways to view time tracking data, including detailed reports, graphs, and a calendar view.

The resource allocation features in Monday.com are also very powerful. Users can assign specific resources to tasks, or allocate resources based on the difficulty of the task. Monday.com also offers a variety of ways to view resource allocation data, including detailed reports, graphs, and a calendar view.

Overall, Monday.com's time tracking and resource allocation features are some of the most robust and customizable on the market. With these features, users can track time spent on tasks, allocate resources based on task difficulty, and view detailed reports on time and resource usage.

6.4 Implementing Budgeting and Cost Tracking in Monday.com

Monday.com's budgeting and cost tracking features allow users to see where their money is going and track their spending over time. Users can create budgets for specific projects or time periods, and track their actual spending against their budget. This allows users to see where they are over or under budget, and make adjustments accordingly.

Monday.com's budgeting and cost tracking features are accessed through the "Budget" tab on the left-hand sidebar. From here, users can create new budgets, view and edit existing budgets, and see a history of their spending.

Creating a budget in Monday.com is simple and straightforward. Users can specify the name, start date, and end date of their budget, as well as the currency. They can then add line items to their budget, specifying the name, amount, and category of each item. Once a budget is created, users can track their actual spending against it by adding expenses to the budget.

Monday.com's cost tracking features make it easy to see where your money is going. You can view your spending by project, time period, or category, and see a breakdown of your expenses. This allows you to identify areas where you are spending too much money, and make adjustments accordingly.

Overall, Monday.com's budgeting and cost tracking features are a valuable tool for keeping track of your spending and ensuring that you stay on budget.

6.5 Leveraging Customizable Dashboards and Widgets in Monday.com

Monday.com's customizable dashboards and widgets are a great way to make the most out of the data you have stored in the platform. With a few clicks, you can create beautiful, informative charts and graphs that will help you better understand your data and make better decisions.

There are a few things to keep in mind when using dashboards and widgets:

1. Make sure you have the data you need before you start. Dashboards and widgets are only as good as the data you have to work with. If you don't have complete or accurate data, your dashboard or widget will be of little use.

2. Take the time to understand the different types of dashboards and widgets available. There are many different options, and each has its own strengths and weaknesses. Choose the ones that best fit your needs.

3. Be careful not to overload your dashboard or widget with too much information. Keep it focused and relevant, and make sure it's easy to understand at a glance.

4. Use colors and other visual cues to help highlight important information.

5. Make sure your dashboard or widget is updated regularly. As your data changes, so should your dashboard or widget.

By following these tips, you can make sure that your dashboard or widget is an effective tool for understanding and managing your data.

6.6 Advanced Reporting and Analytics Options in Monday.com

Monday.com's advanced reporting and analytics options give users the ability to create customized reports and dashboards that provide insights into their data. Users can select from a variety of data visualization options, including bar charts, line graphs, pie charts, and more. Additionally, users can use Monday.com's filters and sorting options to further customize their reports.

6.7 Managing Multiple Projects and Workspaces in Monday.com

Monday.com offers a variety of ways to manage multiple projects and workspaces. One way to do this is to use the My Workspaces feature. This feature allows you to create a workspace for each project you are working on. You can then add tasks, files, and notes to each workspace.

Another way to manage multiple projects in Monday.com is to use the Projects feature. This feature allows you to create a project for each task or group of tasks you are working on. You can then add tasks, files, and notes to each project.

You can also use the Tags feature to manage multiple projects in Monday.com. This feature allows you to tag tasks, files, and notes with keywords. You can then use the search function to find all tasks, files, and notes with a particular tag.

Finally, you can use the Custom Views feature to manage multiple projects in Monday.com. This feature allows you to create custom views of your tasks, files, and notes. You can then use the custom views to filter and sort your data.

6.8 Mobile Applications and Work on the Go in Monday.com

Monday.com's mobile applications and work on the go functionality allow users to stay connected and productive while away from their desk. The mobile apps offer a variety of features and functionality, including the ability to create and manage tasks, projects, and team collaboration. The apps also allow users to access their Monday.com account from any location, and stay up-to-date on the latest activity in their account.

6.9 Monday.com API and Development Opportunities

Monday.com's API and development opportunities allow for a high degree of customization and integration with other systems. The API can be used to create custom applications or to automate tasks within Monday.com. Additionally, the development opportunities allow for the creation of custom reports, dashboards, and workflows.

Chapter 7: Enhancing Team Productivity and Collaboration in Monday.com

7.1 Establishing Effective Workflows and Processes in Monday.com

Monday.com is a workflow and process management tool that helps teams to be more productive and efficient in their work. The tool enables users to create and manage workflows and processes, as well as to track and monitor progress. Monday.com also provides a number of features and tools to help teams to collaborate more effectively, such as task management, project management, file sharing, and chat.

7.2 Defining Roles and Responsibilities in Monday.com

Monday.com is a great tool for enhancing team productivity and collaboration. In order to get the most out of Monday.com, it is important to define roles and responsibilities within the team. Doing so will help team members know what is expected of them and will also help to keep the team organized.

When defining roles and responsibilities, it is important to consider the following:

1. The skills and expertise of each team member.

2. The goals and objectives of the team.

3. The tasks that need to be completed in order to achieve the team's goals.

4. The timeline for completing the team's tasks.

5. The level of responsibility that each team member is comfortable with.

Once roles and responsibilities have been defined, it is important to communicate them to all team members. The best way to do this is to create a document or spreadsheet that outlines the roles and responsibilities of each team member. This document should be shared with all team members so that everyone is on the same page.

If roles and responsibilities are not properly defined, it can lead to confusion and frustration within the team. Therefore, it is important to take the time to properly define roles and responsibilities from the start. Doing so will help to ensure that the team is productive and collaborative.

7.3 Encouraging Accountability and Ownership in Monday.com

Monday.com is a great tool for encouraging accountability and ownership within a team. By allowing team members to see each other's tasks and progress, it fosters a sense of responsibility and ownership for the work that needs to be done. Additionally, the ability to comment on and give feedback on each other's work helps to further improve the quality of the work being done. Overall, Monday.com is a great tool for enhancing team productivity and collaboration.

7.4 Promoting Transparent and Open Communication in Monday.com

Monday.com is a work management platform that enables teams to collaborate on projects and tasks in a transparent and efficient manner. The platform provides a variety of features that promote transparency and communication, including a centralized project management dashboard, real-time updates, @mentions, and commenting.

Monday.com also has a strong focus on accountability, which is evident in the way the platform is designed. For example, each task has a clear owner and due date, and team members can easily see who is responsible for each task. This helps to ensure that tasks are completed in a timely manner and that everyone is aware of their individual responsibilities.

Overall, Monday.com is an excellent tool for promoting transparent and efficient communication within teams. The platform's focus on accountability and its variety of features make it an ideal solution for teams that need to improve their productivity and collaboration.

7.5 Managing Remote and Distributed Teams in Monday.com

Monday.com is a great tool for managing remote and distributed teams. With its powerful features and collaboration capabilities, Monday.com makes it easy to manage projects and tasks from anywhere in the world.

Monday.com's features include:

- A centralised project management dashboard that gives you an overview of all your projects and tasks

- The ability to create and assign tasks to team members

- A real-time chat function that lets you communicate with team members in real-time

- A file sharing function that lets you share project files with team members

- A calendar function that lets you keep track of project deadlines and milestones

- A reporting function that lets you generate reports on project progress

Monday.com is a great tool for managing remote and distributed teams because it gives you the ability to manage all aspects of your projects from one centralised location. It also makes it easy to communicate with team members and keep track of project deadlines.

7.6 Collaboration Best Practices with Monday.com

Monday.com is a great tool for enhancing team productivity and collaboration.

Here are some best practices for using Monday.com to its fullest potential:

1. Use the "My Tasks" and "My Projects" views to stay organized and on top of your work.

2. Use the commenting feature to leave feedback or ask questions on tasks and projects.

3. Use the @mention feature to notify specific team members of tasks and projects that require their attention.

4. Use the "Follow" feature to stay up-to-date on the progress of tasks and projects.

5. Use the "Export" feature to share tasks and projects with team members who do not have a Monday.com account.

6. Use the "Templates" feature to save time when creating new tasks and projects.

7. Use the "Calendar" view to get a bird's eye view of your team's work schedule.

8. Use the "Reports" feature to track the progress of tasks and projects over time.

9. Use the "Integrations" feature to connect Monday.com with other tools and services that you use.

10. Use the "Help" feature to get answers to your questions about using Monday.com.

7.7 Balancing Individual and Team Productivity in Monday.com

Monday.com is a great tool for managing team productivity and collaboration. In order to get the most out of Monday.com, it is important to balance individual and team productivity.

Individual productivity is important for getting tasks completed efficiently and effectively.

However, team productivity is also important for ensuring that tasks are completed collaboratively and that team members are able to communicate and work together effectively.

Monday.com has a number of features that can help balance individual and team productivity. For example, the "My Tasks" feature allows users to see all of the tasks that have been assigned to them. This can help users stay organized and focused on their individual tasks.

The "Team Tasks" feature allows users to see all of the tasks that have been assigned to their team. This can help team members stay coordinated and ensure that everyone is aware of what needs to be done.

The "Groups" feature allows users to create groups of team members. This can be used to create teams for specific projects or tasks. This can help team members stay focused on their work and avoid distractions.

The "Comments" feature allows users to leave comments on tasks. This can be used to ask questions, give feedback, or provide updates. This can help team members stay up-to-date on what is happening with a task and can also help to resolve any issues that may arise.

The "Files" feature allows users to upload and share files. This can be used to share documents, images, or other files. This can help team members stay coordinated and ensure that everyone has the most up-to-date information.

Monday.com also has a number of features that can help enhance team productivity and collaboration. For example, the "Chat" feature allows users to chat with each other in real-time. This can be used to ask questions, give feedback, or share ideas.

The "Whiteboard" feature allows users to brainstorm ideas, plan projects, or collaborate on tasks. This can be used to visually map out ideas, tasks, or processes.

The "Calendar" feature allows users to see all of the upcoming events and deadlines. This can be used to stay organized and ensure that everyone is aware of what is coming up.

The "Notifications" feature allows users to receive notifications when new tasks are assigned, comments are made, or files are shared. This can help team members stay up-to-date on what is happening with a project and can also help to avoid any potential conflicts.

Monday.com is a powerful tool that can help to balance individual and team productivity. By using the features of Monday.com, team members can stay organized, focused, and coordinated.

7.8 Fostering a Culture of Continuous Improvement in Monday.com

Monday.com is a great tool for fostering a culture of continuous improvement. By providing a central place for team members to track their progress and collaborate on tasks, Monday.com makes it easy for teams to identify areas where they can improve. Additionally, the ability to create custom workflow templates and track metrics over time makes it easy to see how your team's performance is improving.

7.9 Training and Onboarding Strategies for Monday.com

Monday.com's training and onboarding strategies are designed to help new team members get up to speed quickly and efficiently. The company offers a variety of resources, including video tutorials, how-to guides, and live webinars. New users are also encouraged to join the Monday.com community, where they can ask questions and get advice from experienced users.

The company offers a free trial period for new users, so they can explore the features and functionality of the platform before committing to a paid subscription. Monday.com also offers discounts for teams who sign up for annual plans.

Chapter 8: Monday.com for Specific Use Cases (Part 1)

8.1 Project Management and Task Tracking in Monday.com

Monday.com's project management and task tracking features are some of the most robust and comprehensive in the industry. With Monday.com, users can easily create and track tasks, assign them to specific team members, set deadlines, and track progress. Monday.com also offers a wide range of reports and dashboards that give users visibility into every aspect of their projects.

Monday.com's project management features are particularly well-suited for agile teams. With Monday.com, agile teams can easily track progress, identify bottlenecks, and adjust their plans on the fly. Monday.com's task tracking features are also very helpful for keeping everyone on the same page and ensuring that tasks are completed on time.

Overall, Monday.com's project management and task tracking features are some of the best in the industry. If you are looking for a tool that can help

you manage your projects and tasks, Monday.com
is a great option.

8.2 Agile and Scrum Methodologies in Monday.com

Monday.com's agile and scrum methodology is
based on the principle of continuous improvement,
which means that the team is constantly looking
for ways to improve the process and the product.
The team is self-organized and self-managed, and
they work in short sprints to deliver the product
incrementally. The product owner is responsible
for setting the priorities for the team, and the team
decides how best to achieve the objectives. The
team members are also responsible for
communicating with each other and with the
stakeholders to ensure that everyone is on the
same page.

8.3 Marketing Campaign Planning and Execution in Monday.com

Monday.com's marketing campaign planning and
execution is based on the following principles:

1. Define your audience

2. Segment your audience

3. Develop targeted messages

4. Create a campaign schedule

5. Implement and track your campaign

1. Define your audience

The first step in any marketing campaign is to define your audience. Who are you trying to reach with your campaign? What are their needs and wants? What are their demographics?

2. Segment your audience

Once you have defined your audience, the next step is to segment them. This means breaking them down into smaller groups based on shared characteristics. For example, you might segment your audience by age, location, or interests.

3. Develop targeted messages

Once you have segmented your audience, you can then develop targeted messages for each segment. This ensures that your campaign is relevant to each group of people you are trying to reach.

4. Create a campaign schedule

The next step is to create a campaign schedule. This includes deciding what channels you will use to reach your audience, what messages you will send, and when you will send them.

5. Implement and track your campaign

Once you have created your campaign schedule, the next step is to implement and track it. This means making sure that your campaign is running on time and on budget, and that you are tracking its progress.

8.4 Sales Pipeline Management and CRM Integration in Monday.com

Monday.com's Sales Pipeline Management and CRM Integration is a great tool for sales teams. It allows them to see the entire sales pipeline in one place, and track progress and performance. Additionally, it provides a way to integrate with CRM systems, so that sales data can be seamlessly shared between the two platforms. This can save a lot of time and effort for sales teams, and help them to close more deals.

8.5 HR and Recruitment Processes with Monday.com in Monday.com

Monday.com's HR and recruitment process is designed to help organizations find, attract, and hire the best talent. The process begins with creating a job posting, which is then distributed to job boards and social media sites. Monday.com also offers a candidate sourcing service, which helps organizations identify and contact potential candidates. Once candidates have been identified, Monday.com's screening and assessment tools can be used to evaluate their skills and qualifications. Finally, Monday.com's offer management tool can be used to create and track job offers.

8.6 Event Planning and Coordination in Monday.com

Monday.com's event planning and coordination features are some of the most robust and user-friendly on the market. WithMonday.com, you can easily create and manage events, invite attendees, track RSVPs, and send out reminders. Plus, the platform makes it easy to share event details and files with attendees, and to keep everyone on the same page.

Monday.com's event planning features are particularly well-suited for businesses and organizations that need to coordinate large-scale events. With the platform, you can easily create and manage events with hundreds or even thousands of attendees. Plus, Monday.com's RSVP tracking features make it easy to keep track of who is coming to your event and who is not.

If you're looking for a comprehensive and user-friendly event planning and coordination solution, Monday.com is a great option to consider.

8.7 Content Creation and Editorial Calendars in Monday.com

Monday.com's Content Creation and Editorial Calendars are designed to help users plan and organize their content marketing efforts. The calendars provide a place to track ideas, assignments, and deadlines, as well as to collaborate with team members on content creation. The calendars can be customized to fit the needs of any content marketing team, and they can be used to manage both small-scale and large-scale content marketing campaigns.

8.8 IT and Software Development Workflows in Monday.com

Monday.com's IT and Software Development Workflows are designed to help teams manage their work more efficiently and effectively. They provide a flexible and powerful way to track and manage work, while also allowing for collaboration and communication between team members. Monday.com's IT and Software Development Workflows are designed to help teams manage their work more efficiently and effectively. They provide a flexible and powerful way to track and manage work, while also allowing for collaboration and communication between team members.

Monday.com's IT and Software Development Workflows are designed to help teams manage their work more efficiently and effectively. They provide a flexible and powerful way to track and manage work, while also allowing for collaboration and communication between team members.

The IT and Software Development Workflows in Monday.com help teams to:

- Track and manage their work
- Collaborate and communicate with team members
- Stay organized and efficient

Monday.com's IT and Software Development Workflows are designed to help teams manage their work more efficiently and effectively. They provide a flexible and powerful way to track and manage work, while also allowing for collaboration and communication between team members.

The IT and Software Development Workflows in Monday.com help teams to:

- Track and manage their work
- Collaborate and communicate with team members
- Stay organized and efficient

8.9 Customer Support and Issue Tracking in Monday.com

Monday.com's customer support and issue tracking are top-notch. They offer a wide variety of resources to help you get the most out of their product, including a comprehensive knowledge base, video tutorials, and email support.

If you need help with something specific, their customer support team is always happy to lend a hand. They're quick to respond to tickets and always go the extra mile to help you resolve your issue.

Monday.com also offers an excellent issue tracking system. You can easily submit and track bugs and feature requests using their online portal. Their team is very responsive and takes your feedback seriously.

Overall, Monday.com's customer support and issue tracking are some of the best in the business. If you need help with anything, they're always happy to lend a hand.

Chapter 9: Monday.com for Specific Use Cases (Part 2)

9.1 Construction and Facilities Management in Monday.com

Monday.com's construction and facilities management features are some of the most robust and comprehensive in the project management software space. With Monday.com, you can manage your construction projects from start to finish, including all the necessary documentation, scheduling, and communication tools.

Monday.com's construction project management features include:

- A dedicated construction project management template to help you get started
- The ability to track and manage construction contracts
- A document management system for construction documents
- A project schedule tool to help you plan and track construction milestones
- A communication tool for construction teams

- A construction budgeting tool
- A construction invoicing tool

Monday.com's facilities management features include:

- A dedicated facilities management template to help you get started
- The ability to track and manage facilities contracts
- A document management system for facilities documents
- A project schedule tool to help you plan and track facilities milestones
- A communication tool for facilities teams
- A facilities budgeting tool
- A facilities invoicing tool

With Monday.com, you can easily manage all aspects of your construction and facilities projects from start to finish.

9.2 Nonprofit and Fundraising Operations in Monday.com

Monday.com's nonprofit and fundraising operations are designed to help organizations manage their fundraising efforts and track their progress. The software provides users with tools to create and track fundraising campaigns, track donations, and manage donor information. Additionally, Monday.com offers reporting and analytics features to help users measure and optimize their fundraising efforts.

9.3 Research and Data Analysis Projects in Monday.com

Monday.com is a great tool for managing research and data analysis projects. The platform provides users with a variety of features and tools that make it easy to track progress, manage tasks, and collaborate with team members.

The project management features in Monday.com are particularly useful for research and data analysis projects. The platform allows users to create project timelines, track milestones, and assign tasks to team members. This makes it easy to keep track of progress and ensure that tasks are completed on time.

The collaboration features in Monday.com are also valuable for research and data analysis projects. The platform allows users to share files, leave comments, and @mention team members in conversations. This makes it easy to collaborate on projects and ensure that everyone is on the same page.

Overall, Monday.com is a great tool for managing research and data analysis projects. The platform's features and tools make it easy to track progress, manage tasks, and collaborate with team members.

9.4 Education and Classroom Management in Monday.com

Monday.com's education and classroom management features are designed to help educators manage their classrooms more effectively. The features include a class management interface, a gradebook, a student management system, and a learning management system. The class management interface allows educators to create and manage their classes, add and remove students, and track class progress. The gradebook allows educators to track student progress and performance. The student management system allows educators to manage student accounts, track attendance, and monitor student behavior. The learning management system allows educators to create and manage courses, track student progress, and assess student performance.

9.5 Legal and Case Management Workflows in Monday.com

Monday.com's legal and case management workflows are designed to help you manage your legal cases more efficiently. Our workflows can help you keep track of important case information, deadlines, and communications. We also provide tools to help you collaborate with your team and clients.

9.6 Real Estate Property and Lease Management in Monday.com

Monday.com's Real Estate Property and Lease Management features are designed to help landlords and property managers keep track of their properties, leases, and tenants. The features include a property management dashboard, a lease management system, and a tenant management system.

The property management dashboard allows landlords and property managers to see an overview of their properties, leases, and tenants. They can also add new properties, edit property information, and view property reports.

The lease management system allows landlords and property managers to create and manage leases. They can also add new tenants, view lease reports, and track rent payments.

The tenant management system allows landlords and property managers to view tenant information, add new tenants, and edit tenant information.

9.7 Manufacturing and Supply Chain Operations in Monday.com

Monday.com's Manufacturing and Supply Chain Operations allow you to manage and monitor your manufacturing and supply chain processes in one place. You can use Monday.com to track your production progress, manage your inventory, and monitor your supply chain performance.

Monday.com's Manufacturing and Supply Chain Operations are designed to help you optimize your manufacturing and supply chain processes.

9.8 Healthcare and Patient Care Coordination in Monday.com

Monday.com is a cloud-based project management tool that enables healthcare and patient care coordinators to manage their projects and workflows in a more efficient and organized manner. The tool provides a centralized platform for coordinating all aspects of healthcare and patient care, from appointments and scheduling to treatment plans and billing. Monday.com's features include a drag-and-drop interface, real-time updates, and customizable views. This makes it easy for coordinators to keep track of every aspect of their projects and workflows, and to make changes and adjustments as needed. Monday.com also offers a mobile app, which allows coordinators to access their projects and workflows on the go.

9.9 Customizing Monday.com for Unique Use Cases

Monday.com is a highly customizable platform that can be adapted to a wide variety of unique use cases. In this chapter, we will explore some specific examples of how Monday.com can be customized to meet the needs of specific users and organizations.

For example, Monday.com can be customized to track the progress of specific projects or tasks. This can be done by creating custom columns and fields that track the specific information that is relevant to the project or task at hand. This information can then be used to generate reports and dashboards that give an overview of the project's progress.

Another example of how Monday.com can be customized is by creating custom workflows. These workflows can be used to automate tasks and processes that are commonly performed within an organization. This can help to improve efficiency and accuracy, and can also help to free up time for employees to focus on more important tasks.

Finally, Monday.com can also be customized to integrate with other software applications. This can be done through the use of APIs or by using the Monday.com Zapier integration. This integration allows Monday.com to be used with a wide variety of other software applications, making it even more versatile and powerful.

Chapter 10: Tips and Tricks for Maximizing Monday.com Efficiency

10.1 Keyboard Shortcuts and Time-Saving Tricks in Monday.com

Monday.com offers a variety of keyboard shortcuts and time-saving tricks to help users maximize their efficiency.

Some of the keyboard shortcuts available include:

- Ctrl+N: Create a new item
- Ctrl+Shift+N: Create a new column
- Ctrl+Shift+E: Edit the selected item
- Ctrl+Shift+D: Duplicate the selected item
- Ctrl+Shift+L: Lock the selected item
- Ctrl+Shift+U: Unlock the selected item
- Ctrl+Shift+F: Follow the selected item
- Ctrl+Shift+A: Assign the selected item to someone
- Ctrl+Shift+M: Move the selected item to another board
- Ctrl+Shift+S: Subscribe to the selected item
- Ctrl+Shift+T: Add a tag to the selected item
- Ctrl+Shift+O: Open the selected item in a new tab

- Ctrl+Shift+P: Print the selected item
- Ctrl+Shift+H: Hide the selected item
- Ctrl+Shift+I: Show the item details for the selected item
- Ctrl+Shift+K: Add a comment to the selected item
- Ctrl+Shift+R: Reply to the selected comment
- Ctrl+Shift+V: Vote on the selected item
- Ctrl+Shift+X: Close the selected item
- Ctrl+Shift+Z: Reopen the selected item

Some of the time-saving tricks available include:

- Creating items in bulk: Users can create multiple items at once by using the "Create in Bulk" feature. This feature can be accessed by clicking on the "..." menu in the top right corner of the board and selecting "Create in Bulk."

- Using the "My Items" filter: Users can filter the items on a board to only show the items that have been assigned to them by using the "My Items" filter. This filter can be accessed by clicking on the "..." menu in

the top right corner of the board and
selecting "My Items."

- Using the "Recently Updated" filter: Users
  can filter the items on a board to only show
  the items that have been recently updated
  by using the "Recently Updated" filter. This
  filter can be accessed by clicking on the "..."
  menu in the top right corner of the board
  and selecting "Recently Updated."

- Using keyboard shortcuts: Users can save
  time by using keyboard shortcuts to
  perform various actions on items. A list of
  available keyboard shortcuts can be
  accessed by clicking on the "..." menu in the
  top right corner of the board and selecting
  "Keyboard Shortcuts."

10.2 Using Labels and Tags Effectively in Monday.com

Monday.com is a great tool for managing projects
and tasks, but it can be even more effective if you
use labels and tags effectively.

Labels can be used to categorize and organize tasks, making it easier to find and track them. For example, you could label all of your tasks related to a specific project with the project name. Or, you could label all of your high-priority tasks with a "high priority" label.

Tags can be used to add additional information to tasks. For example, you could tag all of your tasks that are due in the next week with a "due soon" tag. Or, you could tag all of your tasks that are related to a specific client with that client's name.

Using labels and tags effectively can help you get the most out of Monday.com and make it easier to manage your projects and tasks.

10.3 Advanced Search and Filtering Techniques in Monday.com

Monday.com's search and filtering capabilities are some of the most powerful and useful features of the platform. With a few simple clicks, users can easily find the information they need, whether it's a specific task or project, or a general overview of all the work being done in a team.

There are two main ways to search and filter data in Monday.com: the search bar and the filtering panel.

The search bar is located at the top of the Monday.com interface. To use it, simply type in a keyword or phrase and hit enter. Monday.com will then search through all of the data in the current workspace and return any results that match the query.

The filtering panel is located on the left-hand side of the interface. It allows users to narrow down the data that is being displayed in the workspace by selecting specific criteria. For example, users can filter by task status, assignee, due date, or any of the other many options that are available.

Both the search bar and the filtering panel can be used together to further narrow down the data that is being displayed. For example, a user could search for all tasks that are due in the next week and then filter the results by assignee.

Advanced users can also take advantage of Monday.com's powerful search syntax to find exactly what they're looking for. For example, the following search query would find all tasks that are due in the next week and have the keyword "urgent" in the title:

due: next week AND title: urgent

Monday.com's search and filtering capabilities are incredibly powerful and can be used to quickly find any piece of information that is stored in the platform. By taking advantage of these features, users can save a lot of time and increase their efficiency.

10.4 Advanced Settings and Personalization Options in Monday.com

Monday.com's advanced settings and personalization options are designed to help users maximize their efficiency when using the platform. These options include the ability to customize one's workspace, create and manage custom views, and use keyboard shortcuts. Additionally, users can take advantage of Monday.com's integration with other productivity platforms and tools, such as Google Calendar, Slack, and Zapier, to further streamline their workflow.

10.5 Collaboration Hacks for Streamlined Work in Monday.com

Monday.com is a project management tool that allows users to collaborate on projects and tasks in real-time. The platform offers a variety of features and integrations that make it a versatile tool for managing workflows.

One of the most powerful features of Monday.com is its ability to facilitate collaboration between team members. The platform offers a variety of features that make it easy for team members to communicate and work together on projects.

Here are collaboration hacks for streamlined work in Monday.com:

1. Use the @ mention feature to tag team members in comments and updates. This is a great way to get someone's attention and ensure that they see your message.

2. Use the @board feature to mention specific boards in comments. This is a great way to keep team members updated on the status of a project or task.

3. Use the @group feature to mention specific groups of people in comments. This is a great way

to keep team members updated on the status of a project or task.

4. Use the @all feature to send a message to all team members. This is a great way to keep everyone in the loop on important updates or announcements.

5. Use the Monday.com chat feature to communicate with team members in real-time. This is a great way to get quick answers to questions or resolve issues in a timely manner.

6. Use the Monday.com email notifications to stay updated on the latest activity in your account. This is a great way to stay informed about what's going on in your project without having to constantly check the platform.

7. Use the Monday.com mobile app to stay updated on the latest activity in your account while on the go. This is a great way to stay connected to your team and your work while away from your desk.

8. Use the Monday.com integration with Slack to receive notifications in your Slack channel. This is a great way to stay informed about what's going on in your project without having to constantly check the platform.

9. Use the Monday.com integration with Google Drive to store and share files related to your

project. This is a great way to keep all of your project files in one central location.

10. Use the Monday.com integration with Zapier to automate tasks and workflows. This is a great way to save time and effort by automating repetitive tasks.

10.6 Troubleshooting and Issue Resolution in Monday.com

Monday.com's troubleshooting and issue resolution capabilities are some of the most important and useful features of the platform. When an issue arises, users can quickly and easily submit a ticket to Monday.com's support team. The support team will then investigate the issue and provide a resolution. In many cases, the issue can be resolved quickly and easily. However, if the issue is more complex, the support team will work with the user to find a resolution.

10.7 Staying Up to Date with Monday.com Updates

Monday.com updates are released on a regular basis in order to keep the platform up to date with the latest features and bug fixes. In order to stay up to date with the latest updates, it is important to regularly check the Monday.com blog and release notes. Additionally, users can sign up for the Monday.com newsletter in order to receive notifications about new updates and features.

10.8 Monday.com Best Practices from Industry Experts

Monday.com is a powerful tool for managing projects and tasks, but it can be overwhelming if you're not familiar with all of its features. Here are some tips and tricks from industry experts to help you get the most out of Monday.com.

1. Plan Your Workflow

Before you start using Monday.com, take some time to plan out your workflow. This will help you determine which features you need to use and how you want to organize your data.

2. Create Custom Views

Monday.com offers a variety of default views, but you can also create custom views to better suit your needs. For example, you can create a view that only shows tasks that are due in the next week.

3. Use Keyboard Shortcuts

Monday.com has a variety of keyboard shortcuts that can help you work faster. For example, you can use the "m" key to create a new task.

4. Use the Calendar View

The calendar view is a great way to see your tasks in a timeline. This can be helpful for planning your week or month.

5. Use the Map View

The map view is a great way to see where your tasks are located. This can be helpful if you're working on a project that requires you to travel.

6. Use Tags

Tags are a great way to organize your tasks. You can use tags to group tasks by project, client, or due date.

7. Use the Search Function

Monday.com's search function is powerful and can help you find what you're looking for quickly.

8. Use the Notifications

Monday.com offers a variety of notification options that can help you stay on top of your tasks. For example, you can get an email notification when a task is due.

9. Use the Reports

Monday.com offers a variety of reports that can help you track your progress. For example, you can see how many tasks you've completed in a week.

10. Get Help from Monday.com

If you're having trouble using Monday.com, you can get help from the Monday.com team. They offer a variety of resources, including a help center, live chat, and email support.

10.9 Taking Your Monday.com Skills to the Next Level

Monday.com is a great tool for managing projects and tasks, but there are a few things you can do to take your skills to the next level. Here are a few tips and tricks for maximizing your efficiency with Monday.com:

1. Use the search function to quickly find what you're looking for.

2. Use keyboard shortcuts to save time.

3. Use the 'My Tasks' view to see only the tasks that are assigned to you.

4. Use the 'Due Today' view to see all the tasks that are due today.

5. Use the 'Recently Updated' view to see which tasks have been updated recently.

6. Use the 'Starred' view to see all the tasks that you have starred.

7. Use the 'Labels' view to see all the tasks that have been labeled.

8. Use the 'Comments' view to see all the tasks that have been commented on.

9. Use the 'Attachments' view to see all the tasks that have attachments.

10. Use the 'History' view to see all the tasks that have been updated.

Chapter 11: Security, Privacy, and Data Management in Monday.com

11.1 Understanding Data Security Measures in Monday.com

Data security is a paramount concern for any organization that collects, stores, or processes sensitive information. Monday.com takes a number of measures to protect its customers' data, including physical, administrative, and technical safeguards.

Physical safeguards include the security of Monday.com's facilities and equipment, as well as the security of its employees, contractors, and visitors. Monday.com's facilities are equipped with security cameras, alarms, and other security measures. Its equipment is password-protected and its data is backed up regularly.

Administrative safeguards include policies and procedures designed to protect Monday.com's data. These include security policies, employee training, and incident response plans. Monday.com's security policies are regularly reviewed and updated, and its employees receive training on data security best practices.

Technical safeguards include the use of encryption, firewalls, and other security technologies. Monday.com uses industry-standard encryption to protect its customers' data in transit. Its data centers are protected by firewalls, and its website is served over HTTPS.

Monday.com takes these and other measures to protect its customers' data. By doing so, it helps to ensure that its customers can trust that their data is safe and secure.

11.2 Configuring Access Permissions and User Roles in Monday.com

Monday.com offers a variety of ways to control access to your account and data. You can control access at the account level, the workspace level, and the board level.

At the account level, you can add and remove users, as well as change their roles. There are three user roles in Monday.com:

Owner: Has full control over the account, including billing

Admin: Can manage users and workspaces, as well as add and remove integrations

User: Can access and edit data in workspaces, but cannot manage users or workspaces

You can also control access to your data by specifying which workspace(s) each user has access to. By default, all users have access to all workspaces, but you can restrict access to specific workspaces if needed.

Finally, you can control access to individual boards within a workspace. You can specify which users have access to a board, as well as what level of access they have (view only, comment only, or edit).

11.3 Data Backup and Recovery Practices in Monday.com

Monday.com's data backup and recovery practices are based on the "3-2-1" rule of thumb for data backup and recovery. This rule states that you should have three copies of your data, stored on two different types of media, with one copy off-site. Monday.com follows this rule by storing data in three different places: on the user's device, on the Monday.com servers, and in an off-site backup.

The data on the user's device is stored in an encrypted format, so that even if the device is lost or stolen, the data will be safe. The data on the Monday.com servers is also encrypted, and is stored in multiple locations to protect against data loss in the event of a server failure. The off-site backup is stored in an encrypted format as well, and is updated on a regular basis.

In the event of data loss, Monday.com has a team of experts who can help users recover their data. The team can be contacted via the Monday.com Help Center, and they will work with the user to determine the best course of action for recovering their data.

11.4 Compliance with Privacy Regulations in Monday.com

Monday.com takes compliance with privacy regulations very seriously. In order to ensure that all user data is protected, Monday.com has implemented a number of security measures. Monday.com is compliant with the EU's General Data Protection Regulation (GDPR), as well as the California Consumer Privacy Act (CCPA).

Monday.com has a dedicated team of security experts who are responsible for ensuring that all user data is protected. Monday.com has implemented a number of security measures, including encryption, to protect user data. In addition, Monday.com has a strict privacy policy in place that outlines how user data is used and collected.

Monday.com takes compliance with privacy regulations very seriously and is committed to protecting the privacy of its users.

11.5 Monday.com's Data Handling and Privacy Policy

Monday.com's Data Handling and Privacy Policy covers how Monday.com collects, uses, stores, and shares data. Monday.com may collect data from users when they use the Monday.com website or mobile app, including when they create an account, sign in, add or edit data, or delete data. Monday.com may also collect data from third-party sources, such as when users connect their accounts to third-party services. Monday.com may use data to provide, improve, and customize its products and services, to communicate with users, and to prevent, detect, and investigate fraud, abuse, and other illegal activity. Monday.com may store data in the United States and other countries. Monday.com may share data with its affiliates, service providers, and business partners, and with law enforcement or other government agencies. Monday.com's Data Handling and Privacy Policy is available at https://monday.com/terms-of-use#privacy.

11.6 Protecting Sensitive Data in Monday.com

Monday.com is a secure, cloud-based platform that helps organizations manage their workflows and processes. One of the key features of Monday.com is its ability to protect sensitive data. Monday.com uses a number of security measures to protect sensitive data, including encryption, role-based access control, and activity logging.

Encryption is used to protect data in transit and at rest. Monday.com uses SSL/TLS encryption to protect data in transit, and AES-256 encryption to protect data at rest.

Role-based access control is used to restrict access to sensitive data to only those users who need access. Monday.com uses a two-factor authentication system to further secure access to sensitive data.

Activity logging is used to track and monitor access to sensitive data. Monday.com logs all access to sensitive data, including who accessed the data, when they accessed it, and what they did with it.

11.7 Integrating Security Tools and Practices in Monday.com

Monday.com's security tools and practices should be integrated in order to ensure the security, privacy, and data management of theMonday.com platform. Monday.com has a variety of security features that should be utilized in order to keep the platform secure.

These features include:

- Two-factor authentication: This adds an extra layer of security by requiring users to confirm their identity using a second factor, such as a code sent to their mobile phone.

- Single sign-on: This allows users to sign in to multiple applications with a single set of credentials, making it more convenient and less likely that users will reuse passwords.

- Encryption: This helps to protect data in transit and at rest, making it more difficult for unauthorized individuals to access sensitive information.

- Access control: This restricts user access to only the data and functions that they need in order to perform their job, preventing unauthorized access to sensitive information.

- Activity logging: This tracks user activity on the platform, allowing administrators to see who has accessed what data and when. This can be helpful in identifying unauthorized access or suspicious activity.

By utilizing these security features, Monday.com can help to ensure the security, privacy, and data management of its platform.

11.8 Training and Educating Users on Security in Monday.com

Monday.com offers a variety of training and education resources on security and privacy for its users. The company has a dedicated security page on its website that provides information on how to keep your account secure, how to report security issues, and how Monday.com handles security and privacy. The page also includes a link to the company's security blog, which covers a range of topics related to security and privacy. Monday.com also offers a number of video tutorials on security and privacy, which are available on the company's website and YouTube channel. In addition, Monday.com offers a security newsletter that users can sign up for to receive updates on security and privacy issues.

11.9 Continuous Evaluation and Improvement of Security Measures in Monday.com

Continuous evaluation and improvement of security measures is an important part of maintaining a secure system. Monday.com has a number of security measures in place to protect data and user accounts. These measures include:

- Two-factor authentication
- Encryption of data in transit and at rest
- Regular security audits
- User access controls

Two-factor authentication is an important security measure that requires users to provide two forms of identification in order to access their account. This helps to prevent unauthorized access to accounts.

Encryption of data in transit and at rest helps to protect data from being accessed by unauthorized individuals. Monday.com uses industry-standard encryption methods to protect data.

Regular security audits are conducted to ensure that the security measures in place are effective and to identify any potential weaknesses. These audits are conducted by external security experts.

User access controls help to ensure that only authorized individuals have access to data. Monday.com uses a number of methods to control access, including:

- requiring users to log in with a username and password
- assigning different levels of access to different users
- requiring users to provide additional information, such as a security question, before accessing certain data

By continuously evaluating and improving its security measures, Monday.com is able to provide a secure environment for its users.

Chapter 12: Future Trends and Advancements in Monday.com

12.1 Monday.com's Roadmap and Vision

Monday.com's roadmap and vision for the future is focused on continuing to make their platform the best possible tool for managing workflows and projects. They are constantly innovating and improving their product in order to make it more user-friendly and efficient. Additionally, Monday.com is always exploring new integrations and features that can make their platform even more powerful and valuable for users.

Some of the specific areas that they are focusing on in the future include:

- Making it even easier to create and manage workflows within Monday.com

- Adding more features and integrations that can help users automate their work

- Improving the mobile experience so that users can manage their workflows on the go

- Continuing to invest in security and privacy features to keep user data safe

Overall, Monday.com's vision for the future is to keep making their platform the best possible tool for managing workflows and projects. They are constantly innovating and improving their product in order to make it more user-friendly and efficient. Additionally, Monday.com is always exploring new integrations and features that can make their platform even more powerful and valuable for users.

12.2 Emerging Features and Functionality in Monday.com

Monday.com is always innovating and adding new features to their platform. In the near future, they plan on adding more features related to AI and machine learning, as well as expanding their integrations with other software platforms.

Additionally, they are working on making their interface more user-friendly and customizable for each individual user.

12.3 Industry-Specific Solutions and Templates in Monday.com

Industry-specific solutions and templates are designed to meet the unique needs of a particular industry. For example, the healthcare industry has specific needs related to patient care and compliance with regulations. Monday.com offers healthcare-specific templates and features that make it easier for healthcare organizations to manage their workflows and get the most out of the platform. Other industries that have industry-specific solutions and templates available on Monday.com include construction, education, and retail.

12.4 AI and Automation Advancements in Monday.com

Monday.com is constantly innovating and expanding its capabilities in the area of AI and automation. Some of the latest advancements include:

1. The ability to automatically generate task lists based on user behavior. This ensures that users always have a relevant and up-to-date list of tasks to work on.

2. The ability to automatically assign tasks to team members based on their skills and availability. This ensures that tasks are always completed by the most qualified and available team member.

3. The ability to automatically create and update reports based on user activity. This saves users time by eliminating the need to manually create and update reports.

4. The ability to automatically provide users with recommendations on how to improve their workflow. This helps users to optimize their use of Monday.com and get the most out of its features.

12.5 Integration Ecosystem and Partner Developments in Monday.com

The integration ecosystem and partner developments are rapidly evolving in Monday.com. The company has built strong partnerships with some of the most popular applications and services on the market. This allows users to connect their Monday.com account with their favorite tools and services. The company is also working on developing new integrations and partnerships. This will allow users to connect their Monday.com account with even more tools and services. The company is constantly expanding its ecosystem and partner network. This allows users to get the most out of their Monday.com account.

12.6 User Feedback and Community Contributions in Monday.com

Monday.com is always looking for ways to improve the user experience and create new features that will make users' lives easier. In order to do this, Monday.com relies on feedback from its users. Monday.com has a dedicated team that reviews all feedback and works to implement changes based on what users are saying.

Monday.com also has a strong community of users who are always willing to help others. The community is a great resource for finding answers to questions, getting tips on how to use Monday.com, and sharing feedback. Monday.com is always looking for ways to improve the community experience and make it even more valuable for users.

12.7 Monday.com for Enterprise and Large-scale Implementations

Monday.com for Enterprise and Large-scale Implementations is a feature that allows businesses to use Monday.com to manage their workflows and processes on a larger scale. This feature includes a number of tools and features that make it easier for businesses to manage their workflows and processes on a larger scale, including:

- The ability to create and manage workflows and processes on a larger scale
- A variety of tools and features that make it easier to manage workflows and processes on a larger scale
- The ability to integrate Monday.com with other enterprise systems

Monday.com for Enterprise and Large-scale Implementations is a valuable tool for businesses that need to manage their workflows and processes on a larger scale. This feature includes a number of tools and features that make it easier for businesses to manage their workflows and processes on a larger scale, including the ability to create and manage workflows and processes on a larger scale, a variety of tools and features that make it easier to manage workflows and processes on a larger scale, and the ability to integrate Monday.com with other enterprise systems.

12.8 Training and Certification Opportunities in Monday.com

Monday.com offers a variety of training and certification opportunities to help users stay up-to-date on the latest advancements in the software. The company offers both online and in-person training courses, as well as certification programs for those who want to become certified Monday.com experts.

The online courses cover a variety of topics, such as how to use the software to its fullest potential, how to create customizations, and how to troubleshoot common issues. The in-person courses are held at Monday.com's headquarters in New York City and are designed for those who want to learn more about the software and how to use it in a real-world setting.

The certification program is comprised of three levels: Associate, Professional, and Expert. To become certified at the Associate level, users must pass an online exam that covers the basics of Monday.com. To become certified at the Professional level, users must pass an online exam and an in-person exam that covers more advanced topics. To become certified at the Expert level, users must pass an online exam and an in-person exam that covers the most advanced topics.

Monday.com also offers a variety of resources for those who want to learn more about the software and how to use it. The company's website includes a Knowledge Base, which is a searchable database of articles, tutorials, and FAQs. The Monday.com blog is also a great resource for users who want to stay up-to-date on the latest news and tips.

12.9 Harnessing the Full Potential of Monday.com

Monday.com has the potential to be a powerful tool for businesses and organizations. By harnessing the full potential of Monday.com, businesses can improve communication and collaboration, increase efficiency, and better manage projects. With the right strategy, Monday.com can help businesses achieve their goals and objectives.

Made in the USA
Las Vegas, NV
17 February 2024

85902133R00075